To: Poet
From: UnSpoken.

UnSpoKen's Words

Thank you 4 your
Support!
I Appreciate the
Warm Welcome!

Glenn 'UnSpoKen' Cosey

You Guys can always call
for EC Poet's - (708-296-8311)

EbonyEnergy Publishing, Inc.
A division of the GEM Group
Chicago, Illinois

UnSpoKen's Words
Copyright©2005
Glenn E. Cosey

All rights reserved and bound in the United States of America. No part of this book may be reproduced or utilized in any form or by any means, electronic or mechanical, including photocopying, recording, or by any information storage or retrieval system except by a reviewer who may quote brief pages in a review to be printed in a magazine or newspaper, without permission in writing from the publisher. Inquiries to be addressed to the following:

EbonyEnergy Publishing Inc. (NFP)
A division of the GEM Group
Permissions Department
P.O. Box 43476
Chicago, IL 60643-0476

Although the author and publisher have made every effort to ensure the accuracy and completeness of information contained in this book, we assume no responsibility for errors, inaccuracies, omissions or any inconsistency therein.

Any slights of people, places, belief systems or organizations are unintentional. Any resemblance to any living, dead or somewhere in between is truly coincidental unless otherwise stated.

ISBN: 0-9755092-8-4
Library of Congress Control Number: 2005922077

Cover Model: UnSpoKen
Photograph By: Karla 'FyreMouff' Armour
Cover Design & Layout: Eros Designs & Sarah Gilge

Printed in the United States
First Printing
EbonyEnergy Publishing Inc. (NFP)
A division of The GEM Group
www.EbonyEnergyPublishing.com

DEDICATION

This book is dedicated to my daughter

Jade

You give life to my poetry...

ACKNOWLEDGEMENTS

I would like to first thank God for giving me this gift of poetry! I hope that he will continue to bless me as much as he has!

I would like to thank all the people that helped me with my publication of this book.
I'm forever there if you need me.

I would like to say thanks for my
EarCandy Family
for their continued support in my personal accomplishments as well as professional.

To all the people that read this book and can now understand that there's more than one way to get your point across!
Poetry will forever be in motion!

ACKNOWLEDGEMENTS

Below are names of very special people that I would like to acknowledge:

JADE (DAUGHTER)

E. WILLIAMS (GRANDMOTHER)

S. WILLIAMS (UNCLE)

T. WILLIAMS (MOTHER)

TANESHA & ROMINESHA (SISTERS)

H. POE (GREAT UNCLE)

G. COSEY SR. (FATHER)

M .HOWARD (FRIEND)

K. DOWDELL (FRIEND)

D. BURNS (FRIEND)

R. MORGAN BROTHER)

L. WILLIAMS (UNCLE)

Spoken-Word Artist **UnSpoKen**
Is Earcandy's Reality Check

EarCandy is one of the most liberating poetry sets in the city of Chicago. They have also begun to reach out to the future, the youth with the EarCandy Youth Foundation, an outlet for the youth to come out and express themselves freely. EarCandy's future is very bright; with a non-for-profit entity for the youth and own a Poet's Outreach Building where poets from around the world can come and share their art with the youth. This will allow EarCandy to stay true to one of their slogans…

"Total Art Through Positive Thought"

Who's Coming? The Poets are Coming?

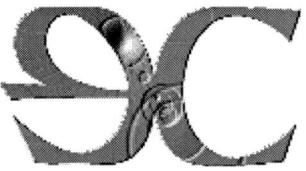

EarCandyInc.

On-Line

www.EarCandyInc.Com

EarCandy is a group of poets, dancers, artists, and musicians exposing art to the masses. We are dedicated to bringing art to the forefront of our community and eventually the world. We want to reach people of all nationalities, creeds and colors in order to share a common goal, expression!

We have created a comfortable environment for people of all talents to bless us with their skills. Our new location, The South Side Community Art Center is a historical facility that supports us in our mission.

We are one of the first poetry groups in the Midwest to open arms to the Youth. Our goal is to reverse, redirect and reprogram the children's negativity with positive dreams visions, and outlets.

"Each One--Teach One"
The battle cry for every poet in the universe…
Without the youth there is no future!

Who's Coming? The Poets are Coming!

Table of Contents

DEDICATION .... *iii*
ACKNOWLEDGEMENTS .... *iv*
PROLOGUE 11
JADE 12
UnSpoKen 14
FEAR! 16
WHY ARE WE HERE? 18
THE ANSWER 20
WISDOM 22
TIME TO STRUGGLE 23
WHERE DO YOU GO? 25
WAKE UP! 26
WHY I'M CONFUSED! 28
MADNESS 32
GAME 34
I'M HUNGRY 35
CHOICES 37
PROMISES 39
DREAMS 41
A POET'S SIN 43
ONLY GOD CAN JUDGE ME! 46
WHEN MY FATHER SPEAKS! 49

WHAT IS UNSPOKEN?	51
COVER STORY	53
LIFE	55
CROSSROADS	57
AM I?	59
FROM ONE-TO-ONE	61
FIRST IMPRESSIONS	63
7-DIGITS	65
DAY 1	66
BEAUTY BEFORE ME	68
UnSpoKen PASSIONS	70
LUST ME NOW, LUV ME LATER!	72
IT AIN'T MY FAULT…	74
CONFESSIONS	76
STRING ALONGS	78
BETRAYAL!	80
YOU	82
I WONDER!	84
MARY	86
MAKING OF A POET!	89
TO MY READERS	92
DISCUSSION GUIDE	93
ABOUT THE AUTHOR	96

UnSpoKen's Words

"THESE POEMS AND MESSAGES ALL RELATE TO THE ONE THAT MUTATES!"

—UnSpoKen

PROLOGUE

This book of poetry is written on the experiences that Glenn Cosey has encountered. It gives an outline of how he adapts to certain situations of the ghetto as well as the world. This book of poetry was not written to preach or teach either! It was written to communicate with
all walks of life!

Some of this material in this book you may not agree with, but for those who understand the points, poetry will forever be in motion. There will be many books of poetry to follow. This is an introduction of an evolution of words we tend to use as a form of expression. This book is a mutation of a human being whose once speaks, but now chooses to be UnSpoKen!

This collection will reveal many forms of expression that is caused by the ghetto, love, relationships and day-to-day life! Glenn has mutated to UnSpoKen in this one. What the next mutation holds will be revealed in his next journey.

Until then.....write and recite your piece!

—UnSpoKen

JADE

I wake up to see you smile
Your laughter
Your joy
All makes it worthwhile
From the moment I held you
I knew it was meant to be
To see a part of me
That's never gonna be shady!
I know times get rough
And me not being there is your fear
I can guarantee it!
I will always be near!
Call me
If you need my assistance
There will be no resistance
UnSpoKen will be there
In an instant!
I hold you at night
To watch you sleep
I'm the shoulder to cry on
When you weep!
Ever since you been born
From your mother's womb
I made a promise to God
I'll be there for you

You are daddy's little girl
And right here, right now
It's my job to protect you
From this unsecured world!
And if that means death
Then I'll walk that path
Watch you from the heavens above
As long as you continue to laugh!
I remember your first steps
As you walk towards me
I remember the first time
You called me daddy!
I remember the first time I saw you
A tear ran down my face
Couldn't believe what just took place
My first born who has fallen from heaven!
I will never forget that day of
August 11th
You are my night
You are my day
But most importantly
You are my Jade!

UnSpoKen

First, Let me give thanks to the Lord
For my birth and thereafter
And show me the difference
Between pain and laughter!
I know it's hard to be a man
But we all must try!
We all must realize that one day
We die!
What we do after that?
I don't know!
I've heard it was places
That many of us can't go!
Why we can't go?
Is a question that is serious as cancer
Look in your heart from the start
And you will know the answer!
What I'm saying to you
Has been said before
Now you must open up your mind
As well as doors!
See lightness in darkness
When others can't see!
Walk straight when the foundation crumbles
Underneath your feet!
I wake up with the world on my shoulders
Faced with problems everyday
I feel that my life is over!
Build up animosity
From society planning for me to regress!
Build up animosity and frustration
I can't hold on no longer

F*** it!
I'm trained as a man
To become stronger!
I stand up with my head up
Vowing not to quit!
Knowing of one love
One Creator
I will always exist!
He's pissed
Some might say!
Think about it!
It's been 430 plus years anyway!
As you see me before you
There's only one Man
But we all share the love
And that's for the Man
Do you know of him?
I think you do!
He's the man that makes miracles and dreams
Come true!
Some call him God!
Me, I call him "G"
He may not come when you call
But He's there when you need!
Now that I leave you
With just merely a token
Now that you know of me
My name is UnSpoKen!

FEAR!

It took God six days
To create the Heavens and earth
And the seventh day He rested!
So why man still needs to be tested?
430 plus years of slavery was tough!
From nigga
To Negro
From Negro
To colored
From colored
To black wasn't enough!
It's rough not only for me
To stand here before you
I'll never ignore you
For me to judge you
I can never do!
When a man becomes a slave
He's building to stand strong
Not a loner
And from the moment a woman
Gives birth
Our generation becomes stronger!

A woman was made from man
So we are equally strong!
Underestimating a woman right
We are morally wrong!
I choose to accept what many can't perceive
Peace between me and you
Is something many of us
Can't achieve!
You say to speak the truth!
But you don't want to hear it
You fear it!
And even though it's about you,
You claim that you don't see it
I'm spoken enough
To let you know how one man feels
Even though it's real
I'm UnSpoKen
Because my lips are never sealed!

WHY ARE WE HERE?

Blood, fear, sweat!
How can I accept that?
With no anger
No fear
As I step through the projects!
The baritone in my voice
Creates a natural distinction!
Never accepted the military
It wasn't my war I was defending!
Front line
Is where they put me?
With a glock in my hand
Now I'm an endangered species
That's walking on land!
Hard-hat, combat boots
I have a souljah desire
Racism, prejudice,
I commence to return fire!
I look higher into the clouds

As the all-seeing eye watches me!
My trademark will embark
Throughout the 2first century!
It's you and me
You never knows you gonna win
I learn to sacrifice and fight
And keep my head up,
When I'm struggling!
I'm steady bugging and keep rugging
On a tragic past
Slavery was a trade of blacks
And dreams of being free at last!
As the road gets rough
The question seems unclear!
Think about it!
Why are we here?

THE ANSWER

Why are we here?
My mind begins to wonder
How can a nation become distinct?
As it continues to be stronger!
I wonder!
I'm blinded by the light
Of the unsung heroes!
Take a trip to the past
it's a trend of superior Negroes
We must uphold strength, and value
That deals with pride
How can we overcome?
We are steadily committing genocide!
It's a long ride
Back to our motherland!
Read a book
Read between the lines and
You will comprehend
Arithmetic and geometry
Was founded by no other
You put us in a ship

Now we're known by our color?
There's no other!
As I embark on new sights
Look through the third eye
Man discovered more than light
It's not right for our history to be erased
So advanced
Back to the motherland
That scientists couldn't even trace!
It's my place
For the question may seem unclear!
If you listen closely
You have the answer
To why are we here!

WISDOM

As a kid, I didn't quite understand!
The older you get, the smarter
I guess I missed that! The older I get,
The more times got harder!
Accepted failure and more failure
I didn't know what to do
I didn't realize there was a lesson
To be learned
After all the sh** I've been through!
You've learn from your mistakes
And you thought you would never
Be the key of that door of times getting better!
They say things happen for a reason
And its reasons we can't accept!
If you're willing to understand it
You'll gain the wisdom that is left!
You learn to swallow your pride
To admit you're wrong
I remain a souljah at heart
and become a leader,
When the time comes along
Wisdom is given, wisdom is to be earned!
It doesn't matter how you take it!
As long as you learn!
Accept what is given, Not what is taken
We are not given many things
And that includes a blessing!
My only regret in life is
Not accepting "g" as a shorty
The wisdom I have now
Proves…He never ignored me!

TIME TO STRUGGLE

It's 5:00 in the morning
Time to start a new day
The struggles I've had before
Go to yesterday!
I pray to the Man for
Bringing me here once again
And without Him in my life
I don't know where I begin!
Its funny how time flies
When you're in the midst of changing
Your life
But sometimes there's a sacrifice
To hold on what is right
As I get older
Time passes by slowly
Giving me the chance to grow!
If I wait any longer
That door will surely close!
Do I have time to think?
Or
Do I have time to look back?
Do I have time to talk about it?
Or
Do I have time to react?
I have time to pray!
But I don't go to church
I have time to make the right sacrifices
Even though they may hurt!
When I was young
I thought life was here just to be lived
I soon learn to appreciate the little things
That came real!

I learn to say what's on my mind
And not keep it in
I struggle hard to keep my head up,
And finish where others begin
I once struggled to get a job
But we all had been through that!
Didn't settle for less
Not even a McDonald's hat!
We all have a different way of struggling,
And that's a fact!
The only difference is...
If the Lord has your back!
We struggle for money
It's never enough!
We struggle to keep food on the table
When times get rough!
We struggle to find love
But we look in the oddest places
Not knowing that there's one love
Right before our faces!
But if we are not paying attention
Through the time it takes for our life
Time is the essence
To make things right!
Time!

WHERE DO YOU GO?

When times get rough,
Where do you go?
When it seems like you had enough,
Where do you go?
Do you run and hide
Trying to seek shelter from the rain?
Or do withstand the pain?
Do you put the world on your shoulders
And feel the strain?
I know there's someone looking over me
It is "He"
And without Him
I will never be
Where do you go?
When it's time to pray?
I say it should be every time
You open your eyes
Just to see another day!
I pray you continue to give me this gift
You see I never thought to touch so many
Hearts and souls
As I give them a bit of reality!
Where do you go in search of help?
Where do you go when there's nothing left?
I don't know!
But I know where I'm going!
Walk straight
Listen to the word,
And "He" will know
I'm coming!
Where did you go!

WAKE UP!

I wake up to give thanks
That I'm living!
I wake up to share this world
God has given!
I know it's hard to handle life
For what it seems
I give thanks to the Lord
For giving me the gift
To dream!
We may go through life with a struggle
But for what?
Its one thing I've learned
That for every turn down
There's a come up!
How much?
I don't know!
Be grateful for what you get
And continue to grow!
I sometimes feel the pain
And realize it's a sign!
He may not come when you call
But He's always on time!
I know when I get to that place
That we call Heaven
I may have to knock on the door
More than twice!
Eventually that door will open
Because in my heart I know I did right!

But, if I go to that place
We call hell!
Let me remain on this earth
Being cursed,
Walk on foundation that won't hold!
Keep me in darkness
Knowing that my eyes are closed!
And if my time comes
It's been one!
But I'd be blessed to leave
A beautiful daughter!
I see what she sees
Imagine what she feels
Now that I've awaken
The dream is real!
Wake up...

WHY I'M CONFUSED!

I'm confused on how people
Get up here and bless this mic
As they begin to recite their verses
They read a couple of verses
Out the Bible
Believe they saved and now they wanna
Curse us! I'm confused!
Why is it when a pastor is having sex
With the whole choir
He's going through trial and tribulations?
But when an ordinary man does the same thing
He's labeled as a dog with no explanation!
I'm confused!
I'm confuse on how we so quick to crucify R. Kelly
On 21 counts
Excuse me, 14 counts of child pornography
Like it's day to night!
But when it came to the Catholic priests
Who raped little boys and girls
And claims to do God's work
Then their reputation is not smudged and
Society doesn't even put up a fight!
I'm confused!
I'm confused on how our black leaders
Go to another country and get on TV
And advocate…Stop the violence!
Come back home and ignore that
Ashlee Poole in Englewood
Three kids in Maywood
One 6-year-old boy in Austin all gets silenced!
And there's no million man march or no protests
On what's happening!

I'm confused!
Why is it we get mad at Bill Cosby for stating
Afro Americans needs to be more independent
On education?
Instead he's being crucified for saying it
In front of nations!
I'm confused!
I'm confused on trying to get money
From the government
And put it back in the same community
Where I lived all my life!
But a person from overseas
Can come over here
Get a job, a house, a business
And open up shop all in one night!
I'm confused!
Why is it that we can't find funding for
Education?
I guess Mayor Daley has us fooled!
But the city can build a 425 million dollar theme
Park,
That features a giant silver jellybean
While the homeless sleep down the street
And many kids and teachers are faced with
The reality of closing schools!
I'm confused!
Why is it that every nationality got reparations?
For what their race has been through!
But us blacks is still trying to get our 40 acres and
A mule!
I'm confused!
Why is it when election time comes
We play deaf, blind and dumb
On the person who runs?

But complains when there's no community
fund!
I'm confused!
Why is it that the economy is
In a state of recession?
Is it because the president is bullsh**ting
The deficit and hanging with the officials
Of the Taliban regiment!
Or why is it under the Bush administration
Terrorists can attack 3000 Americans
On U.S. soil and it's not his fault
He did his best!
But under the Clinton administration
Only 7 died and he's kicked out of presidency
For lying about having sex!
I'm confused!
Why we can't find weapons of mass destruction?
Or is it that they never existed
Or a reason for Bush to go to war
On the price heads of the enlisted!
I'm confused!
Why is it that poets *claim* to support other
venues?
Once they come to your spot
They want to get in free!
And feel since they showed up
They paid their dues!
I'm confused!

Why is it Chicago local artists
Can't get support from their own city?
They go elsewhere
Where the need is greedy
Come back home to represent
But there's no love, just pity!
I'm confused!
Why is it that I can stand here on this mic
And you continue to disrespect it?
Just because I'm not in your clique
My piece is weak
And it gets your rejection!
I'm confused!
Why is it that I made this piece?
For those who choose not to listen?
It's an earcandy piece!
So it's to get you off
Or piss you off!
But as long it got your attention!
And that's why I'm confused!

MADNESS

I'm disrupted by on-going sadness
That creates my own surroundings
Depicted by my own madness!
You say I should have learned
From my outbreaks!
But I'm hardheaded
So there's no room for mistakes.-
Even though the way we are
Some of us don't give
And even though we may struggle,
That's the way some of us live!
I don't live for today
I live for tomorrow!
And every chance I get
I try to avoid the pain and sorrow!
There's no need to try to overshadow me
I'm just blessed to checkmate this game
We call poetry!
The madness I've found
Is surrounded by neglected projects!
What you expect?
A person who's been on his own
Since the age of 16,
With no regrets!
I have much respect
To the way I have gained the maturity of
This game of poetry!
The madness that contains it
Proves without it
You will continue to ignore me!

The words I speak
Only allow those who choose to listen
Walk with no fear!
And to those who choose not
Know by my actions
That I'm still here!
My madness is not craziness
My madness is not suicidal!
My madness is UnSpoKen territory
With un-told truths that becomes vital!
I stand here before you
Creating a mutation that forever lasting!
But another way to see it
Look inside my madness!

GAME

Time flies when you out there
On a hustle
I must show I got muscle
Prove my loyalty
In case I'm bound to struggle!
Everyday is a new day!
As I endure the pain
To make life right
I must be on top of the game!
It's a shame you may go through life
With nothing to live for!
From child to man
The street is all I know to die for!
It doesn't takes long for me to reflect
On how things used to be
Been poor all my life
Until this game was presented to me!
I've learned this game at my discretion
Used it to my perfection
I vocally use expression
As a tool of my profession!
I thrive in the midst
Of my failures being noted!
I share this game of poetry to you
As I've been heavily quoted!
From one to one
Nothing stays the same!
The lesson in this one
You must know game!

I'M HUNGRY

I'm hungry!
As I grab the crumbs of success
I'm blessed
Everyday is a struggle!
Everyday is a test!
A test on how long
My hunger will last
Tempting to make a deal with the devil
As my days slowly pass!
I hear temptation is a reason
Many of us fall
I know patience is a virtue
So I must wait on God's call!
I must feed my hungriness
Before starvation sets in
And without enough nourishment
My journey will never begin!
Where others have failed
I must capitalize and realize
That only the strong of one
Will survive!
I'm hungry to feel the pain
That makes me wonder
Is I'm hungry enough
Before this world takes me under?
I don't always do the right thing
But I'm willing to try!
Refuse to accept failure
Is something I won't deny!
You can accept it

I will not!
I have to pray for what I get
And struggle to keep what I got
I sit here thinking on how things
Used to be
Can't dwell on the past
For it didn't last,
It does no good to me!
From childhood to manhood
In a giant step
Didn't have time to refuse it
Just enough to accept!
Didn't know what lies ahead
Now I'm trapped!
I didn't want to go on
But I didn't turn back!
I didn't listen to people
When I was a young buck!
I didn't give a f***!
But later on in life I realized
That for every turn down
There's a come up
How much of a come up
I don't know
It depends if I became a man
Or
Remain a boy!
I'm hungry!

CHOICES

Sometimes I wonder
If we suppose to live in pain
And sorrow!
It depends on my choices
If I live through today and see
Tomorrow!
We all have choice to make
When we make them it's a given
The consequences we may suffer
Depends on how we living!
I had to make a choice to
Accept manhood over childhood
At an early age
The consequences I have suffered
Made me the man I am today
Strong not weak
Refuse to settle for less!
Intelligent but gifted
All being blessed!
I choose to struggle for what I got!
You choose to steal
You choose to be shady
I choose to keep it real!
You say that you didn't have a choice
The hood took you under!
I've been there and done that

So I begin to wonder!
I choose to be a father
You choose just to be a daddy!
You choose the streets as an excuse
For violence
I choose the man upstairs
And become happy!
And just when you thought
You stop hearing voices
It will be God telling you
You made the right choices!

PROMISES

I made a promise to myself
To make life right
To make more 'cheddah!'
I guess promises are made
To be broken
The more I've tried
The less it got better!
I promise to walk the path of light
But I choose the dark road!
Turnaround in the nick of time
Before death reaches me or
Before I get old!
I made a promise not to lie
In the midst of diversion!
Even though the devil made me do it
It is certain
The man upstairs knows the truth
Behind the curtain I made a promise to
Protect my child and those that
Are near me
Lord, give me the strength!
And I hope that He hears me
I made a promise to love my wife
Through thick and thin
I made a promise
I'll be there 'till the end!
I made a promise to keep a promise
And everyday there's doubts!
I'm not perfect by a long shot
But I'll make the ones that count
I made a promise to God

Not to sin as much!
And in return
I beg for Him to be my crutch!
I made a promise on bended knee
Not to fall to the devil
You know as I know
That's another struggle!
I made a promise to God
I'll walk His path
The best I can!
In return He guaranteed me
I'll be a better man!

DREAMS

I dream of one day being famous
Is that your dream?
I dream of life being better
With more 'cheddah'
Not taking life for granted or
For what it seems
We all may have the same dreams
The way we pursue it
Is the difference between you and me!
I dream for the better
And avoid the worse!
I dream of being saved
And walk away from being cursed!
The truth hurts
But we all must hear it
One day!
The reason we dream is to pursue it
Not to walk away
I'd be lying
If I tell you I don't dream
But I'm hooked
And if I tell you to stop dreaming
Then I'm a crook!

A thief in the night
When visions and dreams
Are hard to follow
But the reality of it makes
It hard to swallow
I dream the end of racism
And that we all are blessed!
And with that vision in mind
I'll take my future to the next level
Be damned to settle for less!
So as I stand here
Making my dreams a reality
I'm on big thangs!
Don't wait to long
Or it will only be just a dream

A POET'S SIN

I write poetry to capture
My time in need
I recite that same poetry
Until my eyes are filled with ink
And my pen begins to bleed!
I need
To feed off energy that unknown to me
Like a pit-bull with words
I mark my own territory!
This is an unsung story of
How a poet dies and lives
By the stroke of a pen!
So let me begin...
By the time I was 15
I would write poetry
That doesn't have any meaning
No end!
It was just something that I did
To relieve the stress of school or
Avoid the peer pressure from friends!
Now that I got older!
My childhood dips from the adulthood slips
And every time I grab a pen and pad
I come to grips!
From no good ass women
Who tells me that they love me
But only wanted me for sex and money!
But it's funny
When you ask for the same in return
They leave you broke and hungry!
Each line I write is a true testimony
Of what I do

I didn't realize that this poetry
Was my escape goat for all the sh**
I've been through
Now back in the day
A poet corner was a place
Where a poet and poetess can get
Some direction
Give a "piece" some resurrection
Make the soul have and erection
Get off the mic and count your blessings!
But nowadays
You have no mic respecting
Poets not getting paid for this profession
And if you're not a big name poet
Then your piece is not "hot" enough
And it gets your rejection!
So here's my aggression!
Let me grab the dictionary
So it becomes my Smith and Wesson
While you talk about the stars and the moon
I'll be on earth
Giving your unborn poetry lessons!
And each time I bless this mic
It's like puberty
It's new to me
And the only way I can overcome it
Is to commit verbal sin
So let me begin!

I can recite 32 verses of spoken word
Verbatim!
Take a page out of the Ebonics dictionary
And re-create them!
Go to Hannibal lector's house
Open up his chest
And feed him his heart!
Spiritually visit the gravesite of
Biggie and Tupac
And get real poetry art!
Leave this mic
Go to another spot and commit verbal sin!
Come back and get the same reaction!
All without stopping for wind!
And that a poet's sin!

ONLY GOD CAN JUDGE ME!

Ladies and gentlemen
Let's see what we can accomplish
Alright?
Let's take you on a flight at night
Let you see the stars that go
High as a kite!
Or I might just kick up dust
And be a 'souljah'!
As I step on this geological, mathematical
Foundation that we grow on!
This planet called earth is
Just a rebirth of what God has
Put here first!
Do you understand my axis on
Why I'm like this?
I think you do
Look at 430 plus years has put us through!
Some say turn the other cheek
Me, I use freedom of speech!
Articulate the words as I speak
Some say "words"
But what are words?
Words are punctuations and definitions
On how we define life!
The cultivations
The articulations
Proves it to be wrong or right!
It doesn't takes long for me to realize
That life is a struggle
In order for us to survive!

It's hard to follow the light
When you are blinded and can't see
I may walk this world
Not giving a damn!
Know only God can judge me!
I wake up planning for a good day
And hoping to see tomorrow
I pray that one day
I rule this world
And avoid the pain and sorrow!
If you never met me
You have no right to judge me
If you thought you knew me
You have no right to judge me
And if you feel what I'm saying is wrong
You will not judge me!
But why?
Why must we be hardheaded
As you continue to judge me?
Why?
You think you are better than me
Then take my life for a try!
And you will see why I choose the path
That's hard to follow
It may be hard to swallow
It prepares me for today
And helps me appreciate tomorrow!
Where will I be never appreciating
What I have or the way I got it
It holds no value to me
Struggling is a part of life

That matures us as we get older
But we never thought it would happen

Over and over!
The way I handle it
Is pure heart and soul!
God gave me this blessing
So I must take total control
As I step away from this thought
I want you to clearly see
Not you, not you and
Not you
But only God can judge me!

WHEN MY FATHER SPEAKS!

My Father speaks as I bless this mic
And do poetry
My voice carries a baritone
Just in case you ignore me!
When my father speaks
He uses words like thus and thee
But told Adam in plain English
Not to eat off that tree!
When my Father speaks
He tells me to walk,
Not to run
And every time I disobeyed
He begins to talk in tongue
When my Father speaks
I begin to tweak and think that I'm
Hearing voices
But it's His way of telling me
To stay on the path and not
Get discouraged!
When my Father speaks
My mind begin to stimulate
My body begins to gyrate
My holy ghost begins to percolate
And my pen begins to write these poems
That makes this room shake!
When my Father speaks
He gives me the energy of poetry
No to hide it!
Like turning water into wine
Or splitting the red sea
I must divide it!
Give the same energy to poets and poetess

I must confess!
For when my Father speaks
I'm blessed!
When my Father speaks
He tells me not to rob, steal, or kill
So I chill!
Grab a pen and pad
And write what I feel!
When my Father first spoken
I was young, dumb, and full of c**
But never nice!
When my Father speaks
He told me that it'll come back
To haunt me
Not once
But twice!
When my Father speaks
He told me not to do wrong
But a hard-head makes a soft a**
And the trial and tribulations
Made me strong!
When my Father speaks
He throws a lifeline in the
Midst of my crimes
He may not come when I call
But He's always on time!
You see, My Father blessed me
Wth this...Poetry gift
So I don't hang in clicks!
Disrespecting a poet or a poetess
Then wait until
You hear my Father spit!

WHAT IS UNSPOKEN?

To be at peace
Means being at peace with self!
And in the end
When it's all done
That's all you got left
We all have choices
But certain choices we make maybe
Unworthy and full of sin!
The words I choose are rude
But articulate
Because I'm **UnSpoKen!**
What is UnSpoKen?
A person pasts and presents
Confronted at crossroads
Mixed inside two worlds
As I speak
The words explode!
The quiet one
Is whom they say we should watch?
As the words begin to unravel
Heaven and hell begins to get hot!
But why not?
You choose to threaten me
With the words you may speak!
I'm UnSpoKen until the time arrives
And my mind tweaks!
And some of the words I speak
Is unknown
I was raised from the ghetto
Don't speak unless spoken to

Or
Get thrown!
You ask why I choose the name UnSpoKen
It's how I perceive the world
If you observe it long enough
And let it come to you
It can all be yours!
Don't take UnSpoKen lightly
For my words are heavy and
Not to be defined!
Take notes of the next line!
One!

COVER STORY

Sometimes I wonder
What this world is coming to
As I watch the brothers and sisters,
On the 10 o'clock news!
I'm glad to see them on TV
And that's in a good way
I'm angry
Of the stories that follow 'em
Each and every day
We all have a good heart
But it's hard to follow
No thinking for today
No planning for tomorrow!
Man kills woman
Woman kills man
When will this sh** stop
When will it end?
Kids dying young with guns
Trying to be Scarface!
Is it their place?
To re-de-fine genocide
On our race?
There's crime on youths
There's crime on whites
There's crime on blacks!
Can you accept it?
You better
It's a hard known fact!
Step back and feel what I feel
See what I see

Open up your eyes and face the reality
You tell me
Where's the righteousness
When little boys commit murder
And sentenced to life or death in
The big pen with big men
Who challenge their manhood
When there's nothing left!
Sane or insanity
You take your pick!
As a young man living in this world
I pray not to die over
Senseless sh**!
My hat turned left or right
Or
Wearing the latest Jordan's or Nikes!
Even for the color of my skin
Black or white
Or
Walking past the projects
After midnight!
It's not right!
But we all must be cautious and worried
Not to end up on
Chicago Sun-Times cover story!

LIFE

I'm trapped 365 days a year
In a cell,
In a 10 by 7
Or better yet……..hell!
Is this what my life comes to?
As I stare at four walls?
I know I'm innocent
But guilty was the fatal call!
In for life with no chance of parole!
I'm better off making a deal
With the devil
Or give up my soul!
I'm old!
As my life flashes right before me
This is a 'souljah' story!
With no guts
No glory!
God told me to walk the right path
And He will look over me!
Where was "He"
When I was faced down on the concrete?
"He" was gone
No where to be found as "He"
Abandons me
Spent half my life trapped!
Now I realized what "He" was telling me
"He" wanted me to follow him
But I didn't wanna step
"He" told me to go right
But I went left!
"He" wanted me to hear the word
And hope that I will interpret!

But I ignored Him like before
And took sides with the serpent!
I'm only human
Locked up as an animal
I can't take it!
I'm shaken
As my destiny was there for the taking
I sit here thinking on where
I went wrong
But I'm trippin!
I had a chance to get out the way I lived
But I was slippin!
My time has come
For it's time that surely last!
As I look through the bars
At the stars
Counting another day that has passed!
I know I will die!
And go to another place
Heaven or hell depends
On "G's" faith!
You may have heard this story
More that twice
But I'm living this story!
For it's my life!

CROSSROADS

At one point
I was confronted at crossroads.
Didn't know which path to take,
Didn't know which way to go!
You may tell me
I'm a product of the environment!
That's bullsh**!
I'm a product of God and that's it!
We may have been born in sin
And that is true!
So why blame me
For some of the things I do
I know it may be wrong
But it's the choices we make
That makes us strong!
All through life
I been told I wouldn't achieve!
And yet and still you believe
That by telling me that
I wouldn't t make it!
I would agree!
I've done some things
That I quite don't agree with!
But I'm hit!
For every time I don't pray
I slip!
I was forced into this world

Now I must adapt!
No time to waste or I'll be trapped
What conclusions can I draw from illusions?
It's confusing!
The UnSpoKen words I'm using
Maybe for some is abusing!
I wonder then how can you judge me?
You can't and you won't!
For the man upstairs has given me a token
Until the crossroads we meet
It is UnSpoKen!

AM I?

Am I my brother's keeper?
I am!
From child to man
Together we both still stand!
I promise to have your back
You promise to have mine!
Under any circumstances good or bad
We go through it!
And in the end
We will shine
Nothing material will come between us
Nothing petty will divide us!
Nothing we can't handle will
Overcome us
We've been through the worse
Time and time again
For so long!
And through it all we became strong!
In the midst of my failures
You were there no matter what
And in the midst of your hardships
I was there to keep your head up
We are men as well as brothers
We share the same goals
Of avoiding the ghetto struggles!
Am I my brother's keeper?
That's just merely a question
Do you understand?

Actions speak louder than words
So I guess I am!
They say blood is thicker than water
And that's no lie
When you miss the water
That's when the well runs dry!
When you miss your blood
That's when you die!
And when my time comes physically
I know I did all I can
Am I my brother's keeper?
I know I am

FROM ONE-TO-ONE

You were my partner in crime
You were my dog!
And in the end,
You were there for me,
When your dogs bark their call!
Now I must walk the streets alone!
Why!
I wasn't there to give my 'dawg'
His bone!
These words are strong
Because they come from the heart!
He was there from the start
And when you seen us
We were never apart!
Where will I be without you?
The first time we me,
We sparked
And every since then as dogs
Together we both barked!
From one to one
We grew up without a worry!
You know!
As you lay here in the casket
Going to a place without me to go!
I wasn't there to give my 'dawg' his bone
When he needed me!
So I guess,
He barks up the wrong tree
Consequences is what I suffer
Repercussions I won't forget!
So...

How in the hell you ends up
In this sh**?
Down from day one
I thought we never split!
I remember the arguments we had
Shooting hoops
Grabbing a 40oz
Sitting on the corner stoop
Laughing, chilling
As we getting blitz!
So for now
I got your bone next to my heart!
For the next time we meet
We'll never be apart!
I miss you!
One love!

FIRST IMPRESSIONS

First impressions
They say they last a lifetime
And now I believe that!
From the moment I saw you
My mind and heart begins to react!
My first thoughts of you
Were mixed feelings
Having it all and being stuck up
Is where I begin!
And from the moment we talked
I knew I didn't want it to end
Conversations got better and longer
Hoping that one day we are one,=
And we become stronger!
You say you are single
But you do date!
So I'm wondering...
Will I be enough to fit your plate?
You impress me with your looks!
You impress me with your style!
You impress me with the conversations we hold
All makes it worthwhile!
You're eager to talk
And I'm here to listen!
At night when I close my eyes
Your smile is what I'm missing!
I know in due time
This lasting impression may
Become affection!

If you're willing to go to another level
I'll meet you halfway
With no rejections!
I can accept you for being you
And not what you have
As long you accept me
For what I give
And continue to laugh!
I've learned many things in life
And learning you may be a blessing!
That's why you stuck out the most
It was your first impression!

7-DIGITS

Hello there lady!
Let me talk to you real quick!
Don't mean to interrupt your time
Take my card
Give me a call for a few ticks!
If you got a man,
Then I'll see my card blowing in the wind!
But if not
Let's start where others dare to begin
You may think this is game
But I'm not trying to show any skills!
Just want time to learn your strategy
And in return...I keep it real!
Sex comes a dime of dozens
And that's not what I'm after!
I rather make love to the mind first
Which takes a different character
I know it's all about houses, cars, money
This is considered to be "big thangs"
I bring more than that to the table
So what do you bring?
It's gotta be real baby!
Don't be shady!
Just want to know you on another level
So as time passes on
You become my lady!
This puts a lot on the mind
As you think on getting with it!
Just in case you do
Dial them 7-digits!

DAY 1

I look at you
And what do I see?
A reflection of what a woman should be!
When we first met
Communication was hard to keep!
No late night phone conversations
As my mission to have you grew weak!
I know you been lied to
Over and over for so long!
I can guarantee you
I will capitalize where others have
Went wrong!
I know these words are strong
But I have no choice in the matter
My only concern is to enjoy your love
Your laughter!
I know it's hard to take a chance
But we do it everyday!
I'm willing to take that chance
If you only meet me halfway!
We wanted to touch lips
To see how soft they are
And you will know!
We both hugged each other
Not wanting to let go!
We toyed with thoughts on making love
But it's plenty time for that
As I drop you off home
And gave you a kiss
I knew where my mind and heart
Was at!

Being true to you is what you want
And you will surely get
But I must tell you
UnSpoKen is not here for the bullsh**!
If you are,
At least I've tried!
If you are
You can keep all your lies!
And if not
I'll wait for your reflection in the mirror
To get clearer!
And that's when you know
I'm very much serious!
On having you as my friend
And my lover
Under the cover where we make love
There will be no other!
I will smother you with honesty
And love that only comes from real brothers!
So as you sit there,
Wondering what should be done!
Ask yourself
Are you down from Day 1?

BEAUTY BEFORE ME

Look...
There you go!
Look...
You re-appear again!
Knowing that your beauty may never end!
When I see it
Can I capture it?
And when I captured it
Can I have it?
And when I have it
I'll adore for keeps
Like beauty and the beast
The beauty in your eyes
Warrants me to make love to you
From heads to feet!
Am I weak?
I don't think so!
I just being stunned by something
I never had seen before!
They say beauty is skin deep
But how deep does it really get?
So deep when you reach the bottom
You're not wet!
When I look at you
How can other not see the beauty?
That God has put forth in thee?
To acquire beauty
You must acquire yourself
Mentally, physically
All with God's help!
And if you got it

Let it naturally show
I continue to flow
Let me close my eyes
As you take my hands and
Guide us to places that
We both can't go!
Everyday I look!
Everyday I wonder!
Every chance I get I ponder!
Why do I chase your beauty as others
Ignore it?
They don't deserve the essence of your presence
Because like you know
I will adore it!
I close my eyes trying to picture
Your beauty!
I can't see
But once I opened them
There's beauty before me!

UnSpoKen PASSIONS

Love
Let us kiss on heavenly clouds
As we search our sexual intimacies
As our bodies desires
The lustful needs of ones passions
Filled with greed!
Did I succeed on making you sweat?
You say not yet!
Let my tongue unveil your UnSpoKen spots
Until you become wet!
A rose pedal leads you to a room
Filled with ecstasy!
My lips begins to cover your body
Down to the inner thighs
"Motionlessly"
Sit back, relax
Don't speak!
Let me get you in the mood
Until the toes curl and
Your mind tweaks!
I believe all good things come to those
Who wait!
If we wait any longer
That moment will fade!
Candles illuminate the room
For it to be well lit!
The fantasies we embark on
We will surely commit!
There's no limit on how much fun
There's no limit on what can be done
T

There's no limit on how
many times you may cum!
Are you having fun?
Yeah, I thought so!
Let me pull you closer
So you can deeply feel my flow!
And if I'm slow
Don't worry!
I'm taking my time to find all the wet spots
We both didn't know!
I'm quiet unless spoken to!
I remain UnSpoKen until my time comes
To caress you!
Close your eyes
Picture what I'm saying!
Then once you open them
Your body won't be the only thing
That's craving...!

LUST ME NOW, LUV ME LATER!

You ask me do I love you
You ask me do I lust for you
And after all this time I thought you knew!
Love is what you're willing to receive
Lust is what you taking for granted
That ends up in greed!
In love
You give without question or
Second-guessing
And it's from the heart!
In lust
You take what you can
With no feelings from the start!
I have a good heart
But it can get ugly
You lust me now
Love me later
All without knowing me!
The love becomes hard to understand
When there's only lust?
So whom do you trust?
The one that loves you or
The one that you lust?
Lust me now
If you want UnSpoKen to talk to you
On intimate terms!

But remember, for those who lusts
Can surely get burned!
Don't get wrong
If you lust long enough the feelings
May get strong!
Love me later
If you can love from the heart
Then the love is real!
I choose not to let the feelings of lust
Override my joy of love!
There are many things in life
We may become expose of...
Temptations, seductions
All followed by repercussions
The abductions of words used are stolen!
The love or lust for a woman is **UnSpoKen!**

IT AIN'T MY FAULT...

We use to talk all the time
But not anymore!
Is it my fault
You got caught as I walk out the door!
Didn't expect for me to see
What I have seen!
You kissing and holding another man
Like you living out a dream!
And if that's your dream then
Live it!
Don't look back
Because I'm not with it!
You've chosen your road,
So let me begin mine.
Keep my head up through this sh**
Because in the end
I will shine!
It's hard to swallow that
You are gone!
But as the man told me
"Life goes on"
We experienced togetherness
But now it's departure
The difference is that
It's much farther!
I thought me and you would never end!
I was that tree
You were that stem
And together we wait for that wind
Not to bend!
We shared good times and hoped the bad

Quickly pass
For I'm a 'souljah'
Who stands alone at last!
With the world on my shoulders
Thoughts of you no more!
Life's too short
I must enjoy what God has put forth!
I was a good man to you
And myself,
That can never be bought!
But later on in life you realized
It wasn't my fault!

CONFESSIONS

I'm placed in a world
Where confessions are necessary to speak
To the unknown!
Transgressions of verbal obsessions
Can be only elevated at open mic forms
Lord, I confess that my heart has written
Trials and tribulations
I confess that every time I bless this mic
It's my outlet to vindication!
For every lost soul that hears
These words
I hope the truth will find them
I can spit poetic rhythm like
A pendulum
I'll blind them!
I confess that many like myself
Uses poetry as their only outlet
To talk about the things that made them
Sad, glad, or the things they haven't done yet!
If Jesus again walk this earth
I'll confess my sins from birth!
He'll put with the devil
Just to prove I'm not cursed!
My heart writes joy for the women
Who touches my life with gold!
My pen bleeds the pain
For the ones that try to steal my soul!
I can confess that the good women
I had in my life
I really didn't treat them right!
So I guess what comes around

Goes around
Not once, but twice!
I confess as a kid
I threw rock at the bus with the handicap sign!
I confess that I forged my mother name
When it was report card time!
I confess on Saturday's mornings
The Jehovah witness would ring my bell
And I would ignore them!
I confess that the times
I did open my door
I'll look at them cock-eyed
Like they stole something!
I confess as a kid
When we play hide an go seek
And the person would yell "all ye all ye in free"
I was to busy playing catch a girl
Kiss a girl in the bushes
With the ones that hid with me!
I confess I would not die for this country!
It would not die for me!
I confess
The day after 9/11
I was seeing Arabs differently!
I confess I don't read my bible daily!
I confess that I haven't been to church lately!
I confess to selling drugs, ditching school
Being rude, not caring what my life is to be!
My confessions is my testimony
That God has never ignored me!
I have confessed!

STRING ALONGS

I've told you there's no end
To our beginning
But inside yourself you are having
Mixed feelings!
We thought by spending time
The emotions will last!
But as time progresses
You say "we're moving to fast"
It was wrong for you to assume
What we was going to be!
And at the same time having me to believe it
While you making an a**
Out of you and me!
I'm grateful and yet confused
On you trying to have your cake
And eat it to!
You tell me things will get better
But it has gotten worse!
It seems like I'm cursed
But this time I'll be dammed
If I'm the one that gets hurt!
You do what you do
When you do
When I'm not around!
Trying to hide those skeletons
In your closet
But they have been clearly found!
Right before us you ask for trust!
How could you?

You sex me...
You sex him...
And now we're through!
I have a life to live and maintain
You can be by your damn self
Playing the...
I'm confused games!
I can't be compared to any other man
As you see
But it's confusing
You pick a man that beats you
Over me!

BETRAYAL!

I have known you for twenty-seven years!
Shed many tears
Every since I was a child
Your voice is what I feared!
Didn't realize your presence
Was much needed than money!
It's funny
You was never there for me
When I was hungry!
I've starved for your love and attention!
But I guess you were ashamed
So...
How in the hell I ends up with your name?
But as the lord taught me
It's better to forgive and forget!
To love not to hate!
How could I do either?
You was the magician who left
Without a trace!
As I got older
I understood what you did
When you did...For a reason!
In the physical sense
You were leaving!
And behind it all
There were your reasons
I accepted this
and moved on
Hoping that one day as
Father and son
We once again become stronger!

Instead,
We got weaker!
There was a time I needed you...
In my life the most!
You turned your back
For a woman,
And did neither!
You showed no love and left me bleeding
With a path of betrayal to follow!
And yet and still it's hard to swallow!
It just proves to me that in the matter of seconds
The heart gets hollow!
I can conceive death
But betrayal I cannot!
I used to call you pops!
Those days are over
So I will not!
Respect is given and
Earning it can be fatal!
I was prepared for that
But not betrayal!

YOU

I look at you,
But do I know you?
I close my eyes trying to picture you
But I don't see you!
At times you are talking to me
But sometimes I don't hear you!
It is you I believe in…It is you who tells me
There's no end!
It is you who is by my side
Through the thick and thin!
It is you that picks me up
When I'm at my worse!
It is you that blesses me…
When I'm cursed!
Even though I may call upon you
Time and time again
You made me weathered the storm
That separates the boys from the men!
My hardships becomes gifts
Your word gives me spiritual gifts!
It is you who has given me this gift
And now I realize that I must
Share it with my peers!
Shed many tears
Of the hearts I've touched
That tells me to face my fears!
There was times when I've doubted you
That was my mistake!
There were times I need you the most
You showed me to have faith!

Basic instructions before leaving earth
Is the book I was given
And through each chapter I've read
Proves
You are the reason why I'm living!
I followed my mind
You followed your heart!
You sacrificed everything including
Your life
Just to give me a start!
You forgave us for our sins
And reminded me what not to do
That's why everyday
I pray
Hoping one day
I meet **you!**

I WONDER!

I sometimes wonder
Where my world begins
If you wasn't there!
And sometimes I wonder if you leave
Could I breathe just regular air?
I wonder will I continue the
School of life
I wonder if you leave
What are the chances of you
Being my wife?
I wonder if I wasn't a dog
Would you have stayed?
I wonder would it made a difference
If I prayed?
I wonder that every time I
Close my eyes
I'll see myself holding you?
I wonder if this dream will ever come true.
I wonder I had to be greedy and cheat?
I wonder why I had you where
I wanted you
But I took it for granted and creeped!
I wonder if I unzipped my chest
And pull out my heart,
Will you accept it?
I wonder if you told me "no"
Could I handle the rejection?

I wonder why I got mad
When the loving stopped?
I wonder if the reason you didn't care
Was because...
I was chasing a**,
At the poetry spots!
I wonder if these words can give us a new start
I wonder if these words are enough
To stop the pain in your heart?
I wonder?

MARY

I live in Englewood
Where life styles change in an instant!
In a blink of an eye!
And there was Mary
15 yrs old
Selling her body
Withholding her cries!
I wonder why!
I can look out my window and she's
Ditching school!
But instead
She opens up her legs
To the next drunken fool!
She runs the street in a cringe
Looking for her next john to spin!
It doesn't matter who goes up and in
All she cares about is the ends!
She has no friends
That she can cry on their shoulders!
You see,
She was molested as a child
So she learn to withhold her cries
As she got older!
Her pain began as an adolescent!
Her addiction to drugs
Was an excuse for **p.m.s.--**ing!
Now she shoots up with
Self-injected hatred!

Opening up her legs to the
Top paid rapist!
But let's face it!
Her heart has been broken
So many times a surgeon couldn't fix it
Her self-esteem crushed
From the tricks she turned
Because they know she's addicted!
She tries to sell crack
But what good did it do her!
For every trick she turns,
Didn't pay her cash,
For she's the habitual user
Now Mary is 16,
With sweet dream of getting out of prostitution!
But having full blown aids
And a kid to raise and
No help from her family,
Made her dreams all an illusion!
Now with this stress
She couldn't find a vein to feed!
Having sex so much
Her walls begin to bleed!
But she driven by greed!
Having countless nights on her knees
She doesn't comes up to breathe,
It's the quickest way to fix her need!
But she doesn't succeed!

Instead...
She sells her baby to the dope man
For an ounce
To hopefully straighten her fix!
But as she didn't know
It will become her last hit!
Uncut cocaine sniffed into the membrane
Her heart is beating faster than
Any locomotive or train!
And then there was silence!
As her body lay peacefully on the floor
Her breathing seized!
So the next time I look out my window
I won't see Mary anymore
May she rest in peace!
Mary!

MAKING OF A POET!

I-am-a-poet!
Committing vocabulary robbery
From the Webster's dictionary
As I transform those same provoking
Cranium thoughts to any UnSpoKen adversary!
I'll carry...
The pen as my pistol
The pad as my vest!
My chest bleeds ink
When there's no paper left!
I am a poet!
Synchronizing meaning in between mental
Conflict
The art of expression is well spit!
Stop hating or criticizing me
For blessing this mic
Just because I don't hang in your
Poetry clique!
Ain't that some sh**!
I'll admit!
Poetry has saved me from
Buckshot after buckshot
From being in jail,
To hanging on the block
At a faster pace!
So it became my anti-drug
Because a mind is a terrible thing to waste!
And my body itself is a poetic feat!
Like from mind to mouth is the
Words I speak
From arm to hand is how

I write this piece!
It's unique!
From the upper-torso
Down to the bottom of my feet
Is how this poetry will guide me
Through the dark!
And if I unzipped my chest
Then you see the words
Written on my heart!
I'll be the spark in the dark
Like Noah ark!
I'll perform head surgery
Without the scalpel
Like Michelangelo do art!
My bloodline carries poetry lines
That multiplies with each piece!
I'll sustain a name in this poetry game
Like flies to feces!
Let's separate the boys from the men
Count to 10
So by the time you reach 5
At your poetry spot committing
Verbal sin!
I begin!
To resurrect and dissect
Any poetry spot that's known to me!
I'll engrave my name into your brain
So horrific
That Hannibal lector himself,

Wouldn't mess with me!

I bleed!
These metaphoric words that we call
Symbolic,
Let's translate the meaning
From scriptures to Ebonics!
It's ironic
That the making of a poet is not noted!
So let me show it!
Like from Martin to Malcolm
I'll mold it!
From Gwendolyn brooks to Langston Hughes
I'll show!
Like a crack-head going cold turkey
I'll control it!
And if you miss this piece
I can rewind it back and flow it!
Not don't get this twisted
You think by disrespecting this "mic"
You think I'm getting off!
But you're wasting your time
I was the last man standing
At Hitler's holocaust!
I can't be brought
Not for the poetry cliques
Not for what I was told
Not for you laughing in my face
talking behind my back
Not even for my soul!
Not even for your mere tokens!
You see this is the making of a poet
And my name is UnSpoKen!

TO MY READERS

Thank you for reading my words. Poetry gives me an outlet that lets me create a world where people are truly free. Poetry gives me the opportunity to discuss the things that makes people sad and glad. Most of all, poetry allows me to encourage people to reach higher goals and achieve their dreams.

—UnSpoKen

Please Email Your Comments to:

UnSpoKen@earcandypoetry.com

Or

Books@EbonyEnergyPublishing.com

DISCUSSION GUIDE
For book clubs, speaking engagements, open mics, literary and special events.

1) What do you feel is UnSpoKen's main message in his poetry?

2) Do any of the poems closely relate to anything you may have experienced prior to reading this book?

3) What views or perspectives expressed by the author do you disagree with?

4) What was your favorite poem and why?

5) How do you feel this book will help others?

6) Will this book help political leaders, mentors, educators and parents in a positive way?

7) How has this book changed your thoughts on society, parenting, culture, racial issues, etc.?

8) How has this book inspired you?

9) What will you start doing differently since you read this book?

10) Will you recommend this book and why?

ORDERING INFORMATION

UnSpoKen's Words
ISBN: 0-9755092-8-4
Retail: $14.95
Volume Discounts Available

www.EbonyEnergyPublishing.com
www.Amazon.com
Distribution: Baker & Taylor
Book & Specialty Stores Nationwide:

If not in stock, please ask store manager to order
ISBN: 0-9755092-8-4

EbonyEnergy Publishing, Inc. (NFP)
A division of the GEM Group
P.O. Box 43476 Chicago, IL 60643-0476
773-445-4946 Office 773-233-5178 Fax

EbonyEnergyPublishing, Inc. (NFP)
A division of the GEM Group

Brings you the best dynamic collection of literature, poetry, prose and illustrations filled with depth, humor, love and life

We are passionately publishing...
One-Voice-At-A-Time
Real Voices by Real People
On-Line
www.EbonyEnergy.com
www.EbonyEnergyPublishing.com

Email:
Books@EbonyEnergy.com
Books@EbonyEnergyPublishing.com

Write:
P.O. Box 43476
Chicago, IL 60643-0476

ABOUT THE AUTHOR

Glenn 'UnSpoKen' Cosey

Spoken-word artist Unspoken is EarCandy's reality check. An artist with respect but without compromise; an artist who "spits" the unspoken words that most dare to utter. That is the artist Unspoken, born Glen Cosey.

Unspoken was actually born in Chicago, but moved to NY at an early age. He has been writing since the age of eleven, and reciting from the age of sixteen. As a child, the young Glen Cosey had a lot to write about life in his surrounds and experiences painted the picture. His poetry became a way he could voice his opinion and make statements, enabling him to say what he felt, while growing up on the "Low End" of Chicago's Southside.

Since his first "live" poetry rendition, at a house party his uncle, Bass player Skeet Williams encouraged him to perform at, he as since performed at a number of venues and events: the Chicago Black Expo, the Spoken Word Café, Afriware, Touch of the Past, Blue Mountain Café, the Blue Lounge, and at the EarCandy set every second, third and fourth Saturday of the month, where he is in residency, are a few.

An integral part of the spoken word poetry band EarCandy; Unspoken, who hails from Harlem, New York, but now resides in Chicago, intends to connect people, from all walks of life. "My job as a poet is easy! The only thing that I have to do as a poet, is stimulate the mind, and my job as a poet is done;" the remarkable artist comments.